THE NEW LIFE LIBRARY
PRACTICAL FENG SHUI

THE NEW LIFE LIBRARY
PRACTICAL FENG SHUI
THE CHINESE ART OF LIVING IN HARMONY
WITH YOUR SURROUNDINGS

RICHARD CRAZE

SELECT
EDITIONS

Select Editions imprint specially produced for Selectabook Limited

© Anness Publishing Limited 1997, 2001

Produced by Anness Publishing Limited
Hermes House
88–89 Blackfriars Road
London SE1 8HA

A CIP catalogue record for this book is available from the British Library.

Publisher: Joanna Lorenz
Editorial Manager: Helen Sudell
Designer: Bobbie Colgate Stone
Photographers: John Freeman, Peter McHoy
Illustrators: Michael Shoebridge, Stephen Sweet

1 3 5 7 9 10 8 6 4 2

Thanks to Iris and Iwa Iwamoto for allowing us to photograph their home;
and to the architects Erikson Associates.

CONTENTS

INTRODUCTION

The art of Feng Shui – which literally means wind and water – has been practised by the Chinese for at least three thousand years. It is a system of arranging our surroundings so that we can live in harmony with them. Although Feng Shui was traditionally carried out by professional Feng Shui practitioners, hsien sheng, increasingly people are learning how to follow its principles for themselves.

Feng Shui can be used to predict and alter situations such as health, wealth, family life and relationships. The Chinese take great care in deciding where a house is built, which direction it faces, how to decorate, how to arrange the furniture and how each part of the house is used. Everything is designed to be harmonious and to blend with nature. This means there should be no straight lines, for example – hence those wonderful curved Chinese roofs. And when you have finished with living in your house, Feng Shui helps you to give the same consideration to where and how you are buried. It can also be used to predict lucky and unlucky days to begin a new venture.

Feng Shui has been known about in the West for the last hundred years and is now practised in every part of the world. It is especially popular in business, where it makes sense to keep employees and customers happy while incidentally improving the luck and good fortune of the company.

The principles of Feng Shui, presented simply, can be easily understood by Western readers as they are based on sound common sense. It is not particularly mysterious or magical – it makes sense that if you live in the country you will get more fresh air and be healthier than if you live in a crowded inner city. Learning about Feng Shui for yourself will help you to think clearly about where and how you live and to identify changes you can make to help you feel at ease both at work and at home. So how does it work?

▲ As we impose our will on the landscape, we have to work with, and not against, nature to find harmony and balance.

▶ A typical Chinese-style house with a curved roof – this improves the flow of Ch'i, "universal energy", and is harmonious and in balance with nature.

PRINCIPLES OF FENG SHUI

A lot of the important principles of Feng Shui are based on Taoism, the ancient religion of China. According to Taoist thought, the universe can be divided into two separate areas, matter and spirit: things you can touch and hold, and things that you cannot. Taoist philosophers called the things that were real Yin, meaning earth or matter, and the things that were ethereal Yang, or heaven. They represented Yang as a circle and Yin as a square sitting in the middle of the circle. This symbol is still considered very lucky by the Chinese and they use it today for their "lucky" money.

THE YIN/YANG SYMBOL

The twin concepts of Yin and Yang were fundamental to Chinese philosophy, in which they were seen not in opposition to each other, but rather as complementary – each needed the other to exist. Thus was created one of the most ancient and powerful of all symbols – the Yin/Yang symbol. This simple but extremely evocative black and white roundel sums up all the essentials of Chinese thought. Each half contains a tiny dot of the other within it to represent the unison of the two.

Yang, spirit, came to be associated with light, day,

▲ This very ancient symbol sums up Taoist philosophy perfectly: yin is the dark areas and yang the light; each has a tiny dot of the other seeded within itself.

◀ Here a Feng Shui master is examining a site to see if it is a good place to build a house. He uses a Lo Pan compass (on a stand) and has helpers to measure the potential site. The river to the south may be too fast flowing but the hills to the north are nurturing.

▲ Lucky Chinese money.

maleness, activity, summer, the south, up and outer; while Yin, matter, was aligned with dark, night, femaleness, stillness, winter, the north, down and inner. The two principles were symbolized even more simply as a single straight line representing heaven, Yang, and a broken line representing earth, Yin.

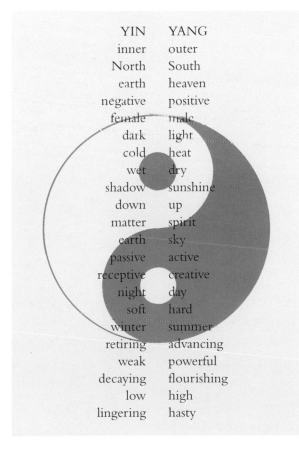

YIN	YANG
inner	outer
North	South
earth	heaven
negative	positive
female	male
dark	light
cold	heat
wet	dry
shadow	sunshine
down	up
matter	spirit
earth	sky
passive	active
receptive	creative
night	day
soft	hard
winter	summer
retiring	advancing
weak	powerful
decaying	flourishing
low	high
lingering	hasty

▲ Clouds represent heaven, spirit, the Yang principle.

▲ Landscapes (the earth) are Yin, the nurturing female principle – the Mother.

THE PAH KWA AND I CHING

Different combinations of these two simple Yin and Yang symbols represented spring/East and autumn/West. The constantly changing interactions of Yin and Yang gave rise to the infinite variety of patterns of life, and this was symbolized in further permutations of the Yin and Yang lines. Adding a third line produced the eight three-line symbols of the Pah Kwa. These eight symbols are known as the "eight trigrams" and are said to have been discovered by Fu Hsi, a legendary emperor of China, who saw them inscribed on the back of a tortoise he found on the banks of the Yellow River around 3000 BC.

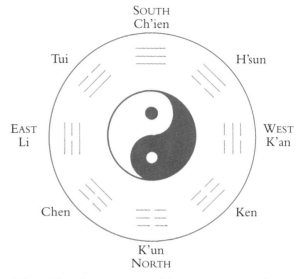

▲ The eight trigrams arranged into an octagon, the Pah Kwa, also known as the Tai Ch'i – the Great Symbol.

▲ The River Lo, where the legendary Fu Hsi is meant to have developed the I Ching.

The top line of each trigram represents heaven, the bottom earth and the middle line is us, humankind.

Later, around 1100 BC, Emperor Wen combined the eight trigrams to make the 64 hexagrams (six lines) of the I Ching or the "Book of Changes". This is not only one of the oldest books known to us but is also still in everyday use as a means of divination throughout the world. The "Book of Changes" is now available in many translations.

THE EIGHT TRIGRAMS

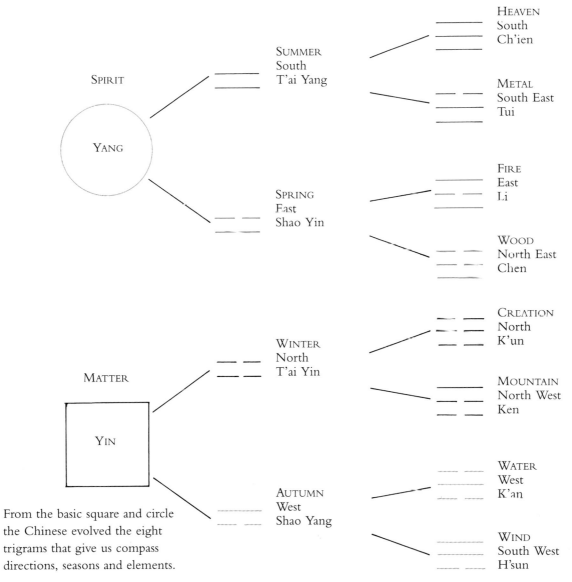

SPIRIT

YANG

SUMMER
South
T'ai Yang

HEAVEN
South
Ch'ien

METAL
South East
Tui

SPRING
East
Shao Yin

FIRE
East
Li

WOOD
North East
Chen

MATTER

YIN

WINTER
North
T'ai Yin

CREATION
North
K'un

MOUNTAIN
North West
Ken

AUTUMN
West
Shao Yang

WATER
West
K'an

WIND
South West
H'sun

From the basic square and circle the Chinese evolved the eight trigrams that give us compass directions, seasons and elements.

THE FENG SHUI COMPASS

Traditionally the hsien sheng, Feng Shui practitioners, were Taoist priests who worked with a complicated Feng Shui compass. This had a magnetic north/south compass needle in the centre surrounded by a series of rings that gave various information, including 28 constellations, the 360 degrees of the compass, the 72 dragon's veins, the 60 points of good and bad luck, the auspicious river directions and good and bad positions for burial. However, a small hand-held compass is all you need to tell you which direction your home faces. This is determined by the position of the front door (or the door you normally use to go in and out).

▲ A Feng Shui compass, the Lo Pan, being used in Hong Kong by a modern Feng Shui consultant.

THE EIGHT ENRICHMENTS

If you are standing with your front door open holding the compass in your hand, which direction are you facing? According to ancient Feng Shui principles you should ideally face south or south-east. This is because your house is divided into eight areas called enrichments. Each area covers a vital aspect of human life. The first area, which is always in the south section of the house, is your fame and reputation area. Thus, ideally, as you open your front door and step outside you are stepping out into your fame and standing in the world.

The Eight Enrichments, with their relevant compass directions, are: fame – south; wealth and money – south-east; education – east; children – north-east; relationships – north; friends – north-west; pleasure – west; health – south-west. In an ideal house your front door would open into your fame area, while your relationships, friends, and children area would be in the north or in the back of your house where they could be protected and nurtured.

But what if your house faces another direction? Suppose your house faces directly north: then you will be opening your front door into your relationship enrichment. This is the area that will receive the maximum benefit or focus in your life. You can see which direction, and thus which enrichment, dominates your life merely by checking your house direction.

CH'I

The Chinese believe that there is a universal energy called Ch'i. As you open a door you allow Ch'i to enter, bringing vitality and life into your home. However, Ch'i picks up residual energy from whatever it passes. If your house faces a cemetery it picks up grief. If your house faces an abattoir it picks up pain. If your house faces a beautiful view then that is what the Ch'i will

bring with it. But don't despair – if your house faces something unpleasant, there are remedies to purify or correct the Ch'i as it enters your home.

▲ The way people move in and around buildings is the same as the flow of Ch'i – we too need to flow harmoniously in curves.

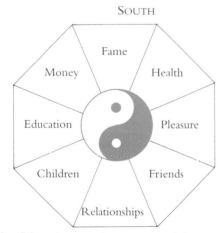

▲ Each of the trigrams gives us an enrichment – an area of life that affects us all.

▲ The seasons change, according to Chinese philosophy, in a clockwise direction, and each season has a specific direction that affects it.

13

THE FOUR ANIMALS

As well as picking up residual energy, Ch'i also has different qualities depending on which direction it is flowing from. Each of the four main compass directions has its own quality which traditionally has been associated with a particular animal.

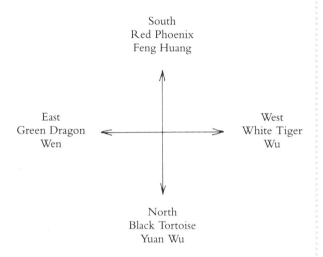

South
Red Phoenix
Feng Huang

East
Green Dragon
Wen

West
White Tiger
Wu

North
Black Tortoise
Yuan Wu

▲ Each of the four cardinal compass points has a symbolic mythical animal to represent it. Each of these animals has its own characteristics.

From the south, the Ch'i is invigorating and lucky. This is the area of the Red Phoenix – the bird of the summer and of good fortune, and ideal for all that fame.

The Red
Phoenix

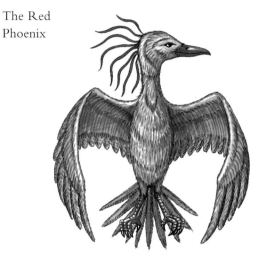

From the north, the area of the Black Tortoise, comes nurturing Ch'i. This Ch'i is sleepy and mysterious, which matches the character of the black tortoise – the animal of the winter. The black tortoise is sometimes represented as a snake.

The Black
Tortoise

The west is home to the White Tiger. This Ch'i is unpredictable and can be disruptive – great if you like adventure and surprises.

The White Tiger

The east is the quarter of the Green (or Golden) Dragon. From it comes protective, kind Ch'i, which brings wisdom and culture. This is why you should have your education enrichment in the east.

The Green (or Golden) Dragon

The four colours of these animals – red, black, white and green – have great significance.

Ideally you would have low hills to the west to lessen the power of the White Tiger and good sloping Dragon hills to the east to get as much wise Ch'i as possible flowing down towards the house. To the south there should be a flat open view, preferably with a stream, to encourage all that invigorating Ch'i. And to the north more hills – even mountains – to protect and nurture.

CHECKING THE LOCATION OF YOUR HOUSE

To check your house from the outside, you need to know which direction it faces. How is the Ch'i affecting your home, by the direction it comes from, and what it encounters on its journey? In an urban environment you may not have many mountains, but tall buildings represent mountains.

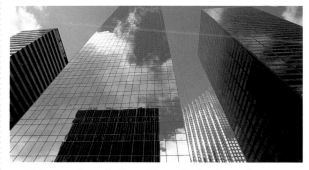

▲ Cities can benefit from Feng Shui – here the straight lines are softened by the reflection of clouds.

THE FIVE ELEMENTS

Another important aspect of Feng Shui is known as the five element theory. Each of us has an element that is the important one to us, although we are all made up of all five. These dominant elements change with the years and are regarded as Yin or Yang.

In which year were you born? What is the last number? If you were born in a year ending in 0 you are Yang Metal; 1 Yin Metal; 2 Yang Water; 3 Yin Water; 4 Yang Wood; 5 Yin Wood; 6 Yang Fire; 7 Yin Fire; 8 Yang Earth; 9 Yin Earth.

The five element types can be summed up as follows:

FIRE: *THE ADVENTURER* – loves excitement and change, hates to be bored, should avoid heat.

▲ Water – the Thinker.

▲ Fire – the Adventurer.

WATER: *THE THINKER* – loves knowledge and intellectual pursuits, hates to be vulnerable, should avoid cold.

WOOD: *THE EXPLORER* – loves to be busy and purposeful, hates to lose, should avoid windy places.

▲ Wood – the Explorer.

▲ Metal – the Catalyst.

EARTH: *THE DIPLOMAT* – loves people and to be of use, hates being ignored, should avoid damp.

METAL: *THE CATALYST* – loves to be precise and controlling, hates disorder and clutter, should avoid dryness.

▲ Earth – the Diplomat.

You will also be affected by whether you are a Yin or Yang type of element. Yang types like darker, cooler houses while Yin types prefer lighter, more spacious, accommodation. This is because we are always seeking the balance and harmony of the other.

Because Yang is light it seeks the dark. Because Yin is dark it seeks the light.

It is the same with the elements. Fire, the south, the Red Phoenix, seeks the cool of the north. Water, the north, the Black Tortoise, seeks the heat of the south. Wood, the east, the Gold Dragon, seeks the unpredictability of the west. Metal, the west, the White Tiger, seeks the wisdom and calmness of the east. Earth occupies the centre and is comfortable with most directions but always seeks to be the centre of things.

You can see why two people sharing the same home may well have two different decorating styles and how knowing which element dominates your character can be helpful

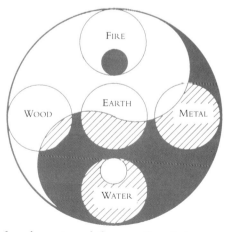

▲ The five elements and the way they fit into the theory of Yin and Yang.

THE FOUR SYMBOLS
As well as the elements, each of the compass directions is also represented by symbols:

THE SOUTH: *THE SUN*, representing the creative Ch'i of the Red Phoenix.

THE NORTH: *THE MOON*, representing the dark, nurturing Ch'i of the Black Tortoise.

THE EAST: *A MOUNTAIN*, representing the vastness of the Dragon.

THE WEST: *A LAKE*, representing the unpredictable power of the White Tiger.

If you look at any ancient Chinese art you will see these four symbols occurring repeatedly. They are regarded as very lucky.

▲ The sun – Summer– South.

▲ The moon – Winter – North.

▲ The mountains – Spring – East.

▲ The lake – Autumn – West.

PRACTICAL FENG SHUI

The concepts of Feng Shui were developed in China thousands of years ago and have remained constant ever since. Where once people lived among mountains and rivers, we now have skyscrapers and roads; where once they looked out on rural fields and open country, we now have parks and suburban landscapes. But the basic principles behind Feng Shui are based on sound common sense, and they don't change.

Practical Feng Shui is a way to put us back in touch with the seasons, the elements and a more natural way of life, without having to escape our modern lifestyle. Mountains (or skyscrapers) can be high to the north and you can have hills to the east, but to the west and south the area should be flat. Rivers (or roads) bring Ch'i to your home. Ideally they should curve gently – if they're too straight they accelerate the Ch'i too much. Worst of all is where two or more rivers or roads point at your home in an arrow formation – this is known as

▲ Even a modern building can incorporate principles of Feng Shui – here moving water has been used to improve the flow of Ch'i.

"killing Ch'i" and can make you restless and irritable. Don't worry if you have this, however, as there is a way to remedy this situation.

There are three important basics of Feng Shui: the Yin – the actual house and its construction and direction; the Yang – the way Ch'i flows in and around your home; and, of course, the middle line of the trigram – you. By checking the Feng Shui of your home you can tell if all these are in harmony, and make changes to the balance if necessary, using the eight remedies. These are ways of improving the flow of Ch'i that have been traditionally used in China, but you may also be able to think of remedies of your own. The principles of Feng Shui can be applied to specific locations within your home, garden and workplace.

▶ A Chinese landscape, with yang sky, yin land, dragon mountain, and a white tiger lake.

HOUSES FOR THE FIVE ELEMENTS

In China, Feng Shui relies as heavily on Chinese astrology, with its 12 symbolic animals, as it does on compass directions. You probably know which animal corresponds to your birth year, and you should be able to work out which element belongs to it by reading page 16, but each animal also has an element which influences your nature – a secret side known as your *natural element*.

The elements for the 12 animals are: Water (north) – pig, rat and ox; Metal (west) – dog, cockerel and monkey; Fire (south) – goat, horse and snake; Wood (east) – tiger, cat and dragon. There's no Earth as it occupies the centre of the compass.

If your year element and natural element are the same the two influences reinforce each other. But if they are different you will need to decide which one is dominant in your character.

FIRE *IDEAL HOUSE:* north-facing, comfortable, warm but quite grand, like a manor house.
GOOD INTERIOR COLOURS: reds, oranges.
KEY WORD: passion.

WATER *IDEAL HOUSE:* south-facing, older, more traditional house, like a period thatched cottage.
GOOD INTERIOR COLOURS: black, dark blue.
KEY WORD: imagination.

▲ This house would be suitable for fire types – comfortable and grand.

▲ This older, more traditional house would be suitable for water types.

WOOD *IDEAL HOUSE:* west-facing, unusual, distinctive or individual (a lighthouse, for example).
GOOD INTERIOR COLOURS: green, gold.
KEY WORD: competitive.

▲ This lighthouse, an unusual and distinctive home, would be suitable for wood types.

▲ This modern, ergonomically designed house would be suitable for metal types.

METAL *IDEAL HOUSE:* east-facing, modern, architect-designed house.
GOOD INTERIOR COLOURS: white, grey, pale blue.
KEY WORD: order.

EARTH *IDEAL HOUSE:* a mid-terrace house or a basement flat, but it would have to be family oriented – perhaps a farmhouse.
GOOD INTERIOR COLOURS: yellow, pale green and brown, dark grey.
KEY WORD: nurturing.

▲ This family home would suit earth types.

Here is an example of how to tie the two types of elements together. Suppose someone is Metal (from their year) and Water (from their animal). Ideally they may choose a period home (Water), but it would be ordered and neat (Metal). Someone whose elements are Fire (year) and Wood (animal) may go for a manor house (Fire) but decorate it completely in modern furniture (Wood), which would be unusual.

THE PAH KWA AND GROUND PLANS

As well as the way your home is sited, Feng Shui is also concerned with how you use the different rooms inside it. Each of these will come under the influence of one of the Eight Enrichments. These eight areas, with their relevant compass directions, form the octagonal diagram called the Pah Kwa, which you can lay over a ground plan of your home to see into which enrichment each of the rooms falls.

MAKING A GROUND PLAN

Your ground plan can be a fairly simple outline of the major rooms, but it should be vaguely to scale. Mark on it the front door and the compass direction it faces. If you have more than one floor you will need to do a plan for each one. You need to be clear about what you use each room for – this is the important part – not what it is called. For instance, you may refer to your dining room, but if you work from home and this is the room you work in, then it's really your office or study. Likewise, if you call a room your study but never work in it, keeping all your gardening equipment there instead, then it's your potting shed.

THE PAH KWA

Now you can overlay the Pah Kwa. This should always be eight-sided, whereas your home is quite likely to be square or rectangular. You will need to draw the Pah Kwa slightly larger than your ground plan so that it covers it adequately, but don't make it too large. The shape of your ground plan may mean that one or more enrichments are not occupied by any rooms, or other areas may fall outside the Pah Kwa. If the area is missing then that is an enrichment you are missing. If an area is so large it falls outside the Pah

Kwa then that is an enrichment that you have in abundance. Once you've done this a few times you will not need to draw it but will be able to identify an enrichment merely by knowing where it all goes. Remember that the enrichment of fame always goes to the south no matter which direction your house faces. Your house always faces in the direction that the front door opens and your front door is the entrance you mainly use.

▲ Overlaying the Pah Kwa will show you which enrichment is missing in your rooms. You may need to rearrange the furniture and add plants and lights.

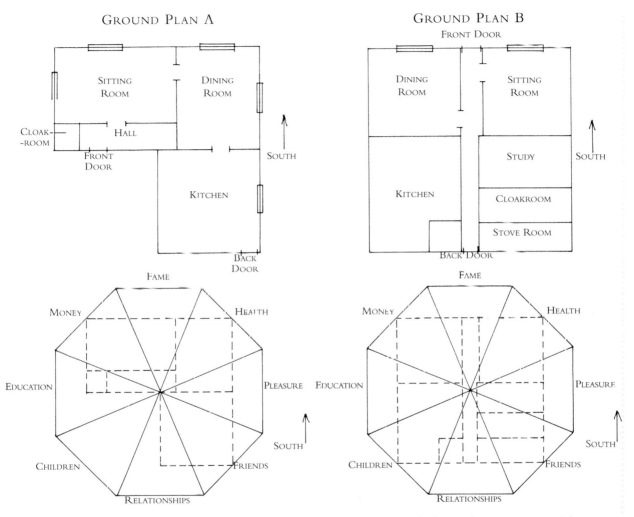

GROUND PLAN A

GROUND PLAN B

Draw up a simple ground plan of your house; you need to do a separate one for each floor.

Once you have your ground plan, you can see in which area each room lies.

Overlay the Pah Kwa with the eight enrichments on to your ground plan with your Fame enrichment to the south.

If you have an L-shaped, or an odd-shaped house, the enrichments that are missing need to be incorporated into your home by introducing remedies.

WALKING THE NINE PALACES

You may find it helpful to draw the Nine Palaces – known as the Lo Shu or "magic square". Draw a large square and divide it up into nine equal squares. Leave the one in the centre blank and fill in the other eight with the eight enrichments. Mark on it the enrichment in which your front door lies. This is your type of home.

For instance, if the front door falls in the relationships enrichment, that will be the predominant aspect of your home. Or if it falls in the pleasure enrichment, that is the primary aspect. Whichever enrichment it is becomes number 1 on the Lo Shu. Number the others according to the plans below.

THE WALK

You are now ready to walk the Nine Palaces. Start at number 1 and walk to enrichment 2. Traditionally there were nine questions to ask but you can ask yourself: What do I use this area for? Am I happy with this area? What would I change? What would I take away?

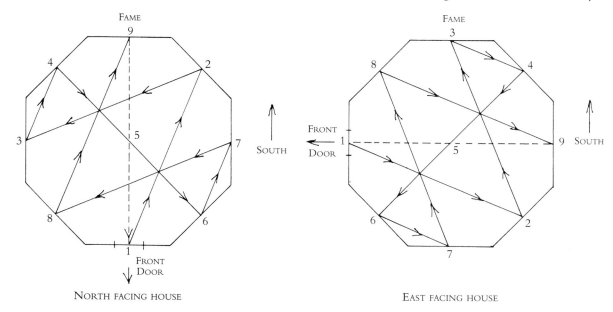

NORTH FACING HOUSE

EAST FACING HOUSE

▲ To walk the Nine Palaces you always start (and finish) at 1, your front door, no matter in which direction your house faces, and follow the walk in sequence, ending up at 9.

What would I leave here? It's amazing what you will see. It's almost as if you are visiting your home for the first time. Perhaps you'll be surprised by how much clutter you've got, or how much needs redecorating, or even how badly used the space is. But remember that no judgment is being made except by you. It's your home and what it looks or feels like has to please you. If you're happy with it then that's fine.

When you've examined each enrichment go on to the next, but do them in numerical order. At each one ask yourself the same questions. It's a good idea to take a notepad and pen with you to record how you feel about each room, area or enrichment as it's so easy to forget later on.

When you've walked the Nine Palaces you will end up back at 1. Repeat the same questions here. You might like to open the front door and ask the questions again about what you can see immediately outside in the world. Some areas will immediately stand out as being out of harmony while others will seem fine. Once you've identified the problem areas you can start to apply remedies.

▲ This very modern bedroom may need some of the harsh, straight lines softened to be truly in harmony with Feng Shui thinking.

◀ As you walk around the room make notes on anything you would like to change or you feel uncomfortable with.

THE EIGHT REMEDIES

For Ch'i to bring you health and good fortune it must be allowed to flow in its natural way – this is in smooth curves and at the proper speed. When you walk the Nine Palaces you can imagine yourself being the Ch'i and ask yourself if you too could flow smoothly through your home or if you would be obstructed, confused, confined, accelerated or stagnated. You can correct badly flowing Ch'i by providing suitable remedies. There are eight of these, and each is best used with a particular enrichment but can be used anywhere depending on the problem with the Ch'i.

THE FLOW OF CH'I

If Ch'i flows through your home too fast it will cause disruption and angry feelings; if it is too slow it will stagnate and cause lethargy and depression. Ch'i likes to flow gently through open spaces, and if your home is full of clutter and untidy areas it will become confused and unfocused. Ch'i likes harmony and beauty, cleanliness and balance.

You should be aware of what the Ch'i has flowed through or near before it arrives at your home, as it is liable to pick up residues of anything unpleasant.

Ch'i dislikes straight lines that cause it to pick up speed and flow too quickly. It also dislikes being trapped in small, confined areas. If you suspect that the Ch'i is not being allowed to flow as freely as it needs to, you may well find that this manifests itself in your life as loss of fortune, an unsatisfactory relationship, inability to relax, lack of friends, disruptive children or even, perhaps, ill health. This will depend on which enrichment the Ch'i has problems flowing through.

LIGHT

Light is energy in one of its most obvious forms. Traditionally, in China, special octagonal mirrors have

been used to deflect unpleasant Ch'i, which is known as *sha*, or "unpleasant vapour". The mirrors are placed facing outwards towards whatever is regarded as incorrect. You can use any small mirror to do the same. If

▲ Round mirrors work well and can be used with candles to heighten the light remedy.

26

your house faces a graveyard or factory then a small mirror placed to reflect the *sha* will improve the Ch'i entering your home.

Any dark areas or corners of your home can be livened up by placing good quality lamps in them. You shouldn't be able to see any bare light bulbs, however. Soft lighting is best to create harmony. You can also use mirrors to encourage light into darker areas or place them at the end of long corridors to slow down the Ch'i. Light remedies are traditionally associated with your fame enrichment.

▲ You can use fruit, spices, herbs, even vegetables; these can all be replaced as you use them or changed with the seasons. This is a good remedy for kitchens.

▲ You can always combine remedies; here light and life work together in perfect harmony.

LIFE

When Ch'i is weakening or causing a depletion of energy or life-force you need to introduce some element of life into an area. Pot plants are best and those with rounded leaves are usually preferable. Cut flowers and dried flowers are frowned on as they have

no life left in them, and plants should not be left untended or allowed to get dusty. Traditionally they have been associated with money enrichment. The Chinese use fish in tanks to introduce life into an area. If you want to do the same you should use an odd number of fish, and goldfish are recommended.

◀ If you cannot use real fish then symbolic ones will do; make sure you have an odd number.

MECHANICAL DEVICES

Anything mechanical or manufactured that does a job of work, or is a tool, can be used to stir up dull Ch'i – anything from a television to an electric kettle. You need to be careful not to overdo this, as mechanical devices tend to be very strong remedies. Traditionally they have been associated with your education enrichment, so this is a perfect place to keep your computer.

▲ If you need to introduce a device you could always try a telephone – it does not have to be too modern.

COLOUR

Any area in which you feel stressed or irritable should be decorated simply in pale colours. White is best, with a single, simple flash of bright colour introduced to focus the Ch'i and keep it vibrant. Colour is traditionally associated with your children enrichment.

▲ A device can be as simple as a pair of binoculars, a camera or a model boat.

▲ Colour can be introduced using dramatic bed fabrics, or you could hang up a colourful hat.

▲ A movement remedy does not have to be moved by natural forces. It can be moved by you when you are in the room; a hammock is ideal.

◀ Movement remedies like mobiles and wind chimes should be light enough to be stirred by the slightest breeze.

▲ You can use colour as paint effects on walls, or, as here, by using plants, fruit, even books.

MOVEMENT

When Ch'i stagnates it needs to be enlivened, and you can use anything that will stir it up – mobiles, wind-chimes, flags, silk banners, even the smoke from incense. Flowing water would be best, though it can be quite hard to introduce into your home, but you could consider an indoor fountain. Movement is associated with your relationship enrichment and this is where you always need movement to stop things getting stale and being taken for granted.

▶ A mobile made from natural fabrics and natural objects can be just as effective as a shop bought one.

STILLNESS

Traditionally in China there would be an area in the home where a statue would be placed to provide a focus for spirituality. This would often be a Buddha but you could use any large beautiful object, from a piece of driftwood to an unusual stone. It should be simple but exquisite and it will slow Ch'i down and help purify it. Traditionally associated with your pleasure enrichment, a still object will allow you many happy hours relaxing and contemplating natural beauty or the perfection of a craftsperson's skill.

▶ Use a Buddha statue to make a good stillness remedy; here it is being used to calm vigorous south Ch'i.

◀ An unusual urn propped up in a corner has introduced stillness to a stagnating area.

SOUND

Harsh noises cause Ch'i to become inharmonious and jangled. You can use wind chimes, bells, even the sound of water fountains to create a harmony of sound and soothe the Ch'i. This remedy is traditionally associated with your friends enrichment so you can play your CD player here and provide your guests with harmonious music.

▲ To introduce stillness into a bedroom with little space you could try a picture that looks like sculpture.

▲ A ticking clock is a good way of introducing a sound remedy as long as you keep it at the right time.

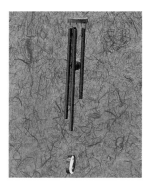

◀ A wind chime will give you both a sound remedy and a movement remedy; this one has a Yin/Yang symbol which is very powerful.

▲ To break up the long, straight line of a passageway you can place other straight objects across it.

▲ You could try a radio by the side of the bed if you need to introduce a sound remedy into a bedroom.

STRAIGHT LINES

Although Ch'i dislikes straight lines, there are times when it needs to be enlivened or interrupted. If your house has beams that Ch'i can flow along too quickly, you can use bamboo flutes, scrolls, fans, even swords to break up the Ch'i and deflect it into the room. Straight lines have traditionally been associated with your health enrichment.

▲ You can use the straight lines of a shelf to help enliven Ch'i where it is stagnating.

RECOGNIZING WHEN YOU NEED A REMEDY

Think in turn about each of the eight areas of your life. How are your finances? Your relationships? Your health? Your fame and reputation? If you are happy with that particular area of your life, the chances are that you don't need a remedy there. But if you are experiencing problems you may well need to do some work on that area. For example, suppose your finances are suffering a bit. You check the area and find that your money enrichment happens to fall in your dining room. Perhaps you've been eating all your money?

▲ Any corner, especially near windows, should be attended to; use plants to stop the Ch'i lingering.

▲ Use a wind chime to open up a window that is blocked off by a sloping ceiling.

If you visit a Chinese restaurant you may well see a fish tank near the cash register – this is to encourage money to come to life. Perhaps you could try a fish tank in your dining room, or a large plant to encourage the Ch'i to provide good fortune.

Suppose that your relationship with your partner is suffering and you check that enrichment area and find it falls in your study. Perhaps you have been devoting too much time to work? If you and your partner are in business together, maybe you are not spending enough time together away from work? You could try introducing a wind chime above your desk to stir up the Ch'i, or even an executive desk toy that moves. If you have a computer on your desk, try running a moving screen-saver when you're not using it.

EXPERIMENTING WITH REMEDIES

The thing to remember with remedies is that you can't do any harm by introducing one into an area. If it's the wrong one you will simply remain static – there will be no improvement. Sometimes you have to experiment and move things around before you produce a positive result.

Remember that Ch'i likes harmony, beauty, order, spaciousness and gentle curves. It dislikes disorder, clutter, straight lines and neglected areas. You may realize that you have to redecorate your home completely – not because the colour scheme is wrong but because decay and neglect have set in. Ch'i likes spring-cleaning and freshness. Sometimes that's all you need to do to an area to benefit from better Ch'i – clean and tidy up. Your home should reflect your inner self. If you are cluttered and confused inside, your home may reflect that. By clearing out the clutter externally you can help to shift the inner debris and revitalize yourself. By focusing on a particular aspect of your life you will already have taken a major step towards improvement.

▲ Ch'i likes gentle curves and this wall will allow it to flow beautifully.

▲ The straight lines of these shutters can hinder the Ch'i; use a revolving crystal to encourage the Ch'i.

FENG SHUI IN THE HOME

Our homes are where we socialise, bring up our children, live as a family and enjoy our relationships – some of us even work at home. Having a home that is comfortable and gives us pleasure is a dream we all have. Feng Shui is an effective way of examining where and how we live so that we know what to do to improve it.

Once you've drawn up a ground plan of your home and checked with the Pah Kwa to see where each of the Eight Enrichments falls, you will have a much clearer idea of what you use each area for. Once you've done that you may not need to use any remedies at all – just change areas for improvement.

It is important that you feel confident as you step out into the world from your front door.

▲ Clutter is stored away in this dining area in a large, well-organized cupboard.

If you step out from a cluttered, dark and badly decorated home you will not feel as powerful and confident than if you leave behind you a well ordered, clean, happy environment, especially one that is a joy to return to.

▲ Use ornamental pots to help break up the straight lines of polished floorboards.

▶ By placing a plant near a window you help the Ch'i to circulate smoothly.

THE LIVING ROOM

Ideally, your living room will fall within your pleasure enrichment. If it doesn't you may need to look at what you use the room for.

In most cases your living room, as with most rooms in your home, will be roughly four-sided. And the traditional Western arrangement of such a room would be to line up the furniture parallel with the walls. Instead, try incorporating the octagonal Pah Kwa shape into the arrangement of your furniture.

▲ You can use an open fire as an effective movement remedy and a picture is a good colour remedy.

You may find that it makes everything seem warmer and cosier. You will be left with corners where you can place lamps or plants, light and life remedies, to liven up any Ch'i that may be prone to stagnate.

In a traditional Chinese home the living room would have a fire as its main focus. Nowadays there is a tendency to focus on the television, which can introduce a very powerful mechanical device remedy where it may well not be wanted. Perhaps you could experiment with "hiding" the TV and video in a cabinet and returning to the fire as a central focus.

If you have a dining area in this room, or if the living room opens on to the kitchen, this should be screened from the living area. You might be able to use a trellis with climbing plants. Watch out for corners jutting into the room – these corners should also be "rounded" off with plants.

Try to keep the room as uncluttered as possible so the Ch'i can circulate evenly.

If you have any mirrors in the living room make sure that they don't "behead" you when you look in them. They should be angled so that you can see yourself clearly.

Whoever uses the room most should occupy the "honoured guest" position. This is the chair that faces the main door into the room so you can see whoever is coming in before they see you. This chair should, of course, be given up for a special guest.

◀ If all the furniture is pushed against the walls in severe, straight lines it will cause the Ch'i to move too quickly.

▶ Use the Pah Kwa shape to rearrange the furniture. This keeps the Ch'i circulating smoothly.

◀ The straight shelf behind the sofa will cause discomfort and the spiky twigs will leak money.

▶ The sofa is better at an angle, and the round leaves of the plant are a good money remedy.

◀ If the door to the dining room opens behind the turquoise chair the occupant is likely to feel uncomfortable.

▶ A simple rearrangement allows two guests to have "honoured guest" chairs and frees up the Ch'i for everyone.

THE BEDROOM

The two important things to watch out for when checking the Feng Shui of your bedroom are that there are no beams above the bed and that the bed is not directly opposite the door.

If you have ceiling beams and cannot arrange the bed in any other way, you should hang fabrics from the beams to interrupt the accelerated flow of Ch'i, otherwise it is said to bring ill health. You could always try a mosquito net, which will break up the Ch'i as well as serve its primary purpose.

Ideally the bed should be positioned so that you can see anyone coming into the room before they see you. By Chinese tradition, a dead person is always carried feet first out of the bedroom, so you should never have your feet aligned directly opposite the door.

As you spend a lot of time in your bedroom it is

▲ A good use of light remedies in a bedroom and a very good Feng Shui bed head.

worth checking out which enrichment it falls into –
ideally pleasure, health or relationships. You may need
to make adjustments if it doesn't.

Bedrooms should be as light and uncluttered as
possible so the Ch'i can restore you while you are
asleep. Piles of clothes on the floor or undusted surfaces are not helpful. The bed should be as high as
possible off the floor and as comfortable, luxurious
and decadent as you like.

Your bedroom really needs only a bed in it – you
shouldn't be using it as an office or study as well. If
you can't avoid that then it's worth trying to screen off
your work area from your sleeping area. The same
goes for any washing facilities in the room.

If your windows don't look out on to glorious
views you can add paintings of pleasant landscapes or
use a mirror to reflect a better view into the room. As
you enter, you shouldn't be able to see yourself in any
mirrors you may have in the room – nor should you
be able to see yourself in a mirror when you're in bed.

▲ Add colour to a north-east facing bedroom to calm
anxieties about children or to increase fertility.

▲ Position a bed by an east-facing window to improve
your wisdom; add some books to increase learning.

▲ Make a bedroom with a west-facing window
peaceful by using fabric to calm the Ch'i.

THE KITCHEN

This is the very heart of the home and can benefit more than any other room from good Feng Shui. Ideally it will fall into your west or north-west areas of friends or pleasure. This is where you will cook all those fantastic meals that will be talked about forever.

A kitchen is not a room for formal entertaining, so you can design it in a particularly indulgent way – it is for you to work in happily and it should suit you. If you are very tall raise all your work surfaces – and do the opposite if you are small. Nobody should be able to walk behind you without you seeing them, so lots of mirrors are important.

▲ Red in the kitchen is a good colour for healthy and creative cooking.

Pieces of equipment like blenders, mixers and food processors should be put away when not in use as they are powerful mechanical device remedies. The Chinese will not use many, if any, remedies in the kitchen as they feel it is already full – of the colour of food, the movement of steam, the sound of dishes clashing, mechanical devices (the kitchen equipment), straight lines along the work surfaces, and the light of flames cooking. The only things you may need are stillness to calm the frenzy of food preparation, and life – but this can well be you and your family, or a sleeping cat by the stove.

Remember that in the kitchen certain elements may be brought into opposition with each other – do not have Fire (the stove) next to Water (the refrigerator), or Wood (the work surfaces perhaps) next to Metal (the knives – they should always be stored away). This is because Water and Fire, Wood and Metal belong in opposing compass directions.

As you overlay the Pah Kwa on the whole house so too should you overlay it on the kitchen individually. The stove (your fame) should ideally be in the south. If you eat in the kitchen try to do it in the east so you can have good educational conversations over the meal. Food should be stored in the west (pleasure) and the sink should ideally be in the north (relationships) so you can share the chores – you hope!

▲ Life remedies for kitchens can be plants; you can also use fruit, peppers, vegetables, even bread.

◀ Keep kitchen work surfaces free of clutter to allow the Ch'i to move freely around.

▶ Here the surfaces are clear but the wastebin should be moved away from the door.

THE BATHROOM

Bathrooms should be bright and clean. Towels left on the floor are not helpful – tidy up after yourself and the Ch'i will circulate better and cause less dampness. Make bathrooms as warm and comfortable as possible and try to eliminate any damp problems.

The very worst thing, according to traditional Feng Shui principles, is to have the toilet directly opposite the bathroom door. The Chinese, like many Asian races, are extremely private and would not consider being seen sitting on the toilet to be a good thing. If the toilet can be seen from the door you should consider screening it. The toilet lid should never be left up. And if the toilet is in the south-east (wealth) you will be flushing your money away - so the lid should definitely be kept down.

Ideally your bathroom will be in the north – a private, nurturing area where you can relax. If it is too near the front of your house it will suffer from the excitable Yang Ch'i entering your home.

Light remedies work well in bathrooms – you can use candlelight to good effect. Life, in the form of plants, seems to work well too, and the plants like the steamy atmosphere.

The bathroom should be kept clean and hygienic – avoid clutter and untidy areas in this room if you can

▲ If the toilet is in the south-east (wealth) and the lid is up it will allow money to be flushed away.

▲ A screened toilet and uncluttered surfaces in a bathroom is good Feng Shui.

as the Ch'i will not only stagnate here but rapidly decay – allowing condensation, fungal growth and damp to set in.

If you use mirrors here they should not be in front of windows, nor should they be too high or low.

A bathroom is a watery place so is best suited to the north. If it is in the south (Fire) you can introduce more watery elements by using pictures of fish or river landscapes. Or try painting it in shades of blue. You can also try hanging a small mirror on the outside of the bathroom door to deflect any Ch'i that's too powerful. See which enrichment your bathroom falls into – this may give you a clue to any problem areas in your life. It may be that any energy is being flushed, or drained away with the bath water, and you'll need to keep the toilet seat down for the same reason. Bathrooms are very Yin rooms and need to be plainly decorated. Any furnishings should be very simple.

▲ This bathroom has plenty of round edges to help keep the Ch'i circulating.

▲ Use a plant in a bathroom to free up any stagnating Ch'i. It is a good life remedy.

▲ Make sure mirrors in bathrooms are kept clean. It is considered bad Feng Shui to let mirrors steam up.

DOORS

Doors should never open directly opposite each other but should ideally be offset. If they are not, you may need to hang a small mirror on one of them to deflect the other. Long corridors with lots of doors opening off them should be broken up with banners or flags hung from the ceiling.

▲ Long corridors can funnel Ch'i too quickly.

Great care must be taken with the front (or main) door to the house. If it's too large or out of proportion it will allow too much Ch'i to enter and you'll feel swamped. If it is too small it will restrict the Ch'i, making you feel suffocated. The front door should always be well lit on the outside, particularly if it is in your fame area – you don't want to hide your light.

What can you see from the front door? This is possibly one of the most important aspects of Feng Shui. Whatever it is you can see will have the greatest influence in your life. If it's positive, such as a pleasant landscape or a beautiful view, then that's fine, but if it's not then you will need to hang a mirror on the outside of the door to deflect the energy.

▲ This front door shows the owner's confidence.

▲ To encourage Ch'i, plants can be grown around your front door.

◀ If you have a double front door make sure both sides can be opened easily – ideally you should open both halves when you enter or leave.

▲ Even if front doors are identical we feel a need to personalize them.

WINDOWS

Windows, ideally, should open outwards. If they open inwards they will not allow Ch'i to circulate properly. Sash windows are frowned on in China for Feng Shui purposes as they don't open wide enough – but they are often wider than a casement window would be, especially in Georgian houses.

Curtains should be capable of being drawn back completely free of the window to allow the maximum light, and Ch'i, to enter. Tie them back to fall in a gracious curve rather than hanging down straight. Windows and curtains should be cleaned, or at least dusted, regularly. Windows with an octagonal or arched shape are considered good Feng Shui and should be left uncurtained if possible. In China any windows that look out to the west are frequently kept with the curtains drawn over them, and it's not unknown for the window to be painted black – this stops any disruptive Tiger Ch'i from entering.

▲ Curtains can be curved around a window to encourage Ch'i to be more restful.

▲ Curtains ideally should hang in gracious curves and fall to the floor rather than being too straight or too short.

▶ You can use heatlthy plants or even crockery to deflect Ch'i from an unpleasant direction.

FENG SHUI IN THE GARDEN

In an ideal world we would have our garden on all four sides of our house. In this ideal garden, we could have a beautiful lawn to the south to encourage our fame, a high mountain to the north to nurture and protect us, good hills to the east to encourage the wisdom of the Dragon, and a gentle lake to the west to keep the Tiger at bay. However, most of us have to settle for a small front garden and a larger back one – if we even manage to get that. Some of us have only a humble window box to keep us in touch with nature.

▲ You can use mixed lavenders to help slow Ch'i down along fences and straight paths.

▲ Use climbing roses to help break up harsh lines and encourage the Ch'i to circulate gently.

But the principles of good Feng Shui stay the same whether you are cultivating a large park or a shrub in a tub – there must be curves, curves and more curves. Nothing must be too large or too small, but everything in proportion.

If you like, you can think of your house as the Yin aspect and your garden as the Yang. Yang is all to do with light and space. In the West we think a garden is finished when we can't fit any more plants into it, but in China a garden is finished when you can't take anything else away. Everybody has probably heard of, or seen, Japanese Zen gardens, but they originated in China, where gardens have been cultivated since at least the 6th century BC.

▶ The seated Buddha, lilies and bamboo are all very good Feng Shui elements to have in your garden.

GARDEN ELEMENTS

The ideal garden to aim for contains a little of each of the five elements: a pond or pool for Water, a sundial or bronze statue for Metal, trees and shrubs for Wood, lots of red and orange colours for Fire and earth for Earth.

There should be a place to sit in contemplation, a place to eat, hidden areas for surprise and excitement, and walkways to stroll through.

Compost heaps, dustbins (trash cans) and fuel storage bins should all be hidden: screen them with trellis covered in climbers if you can or, failing that, grow shrubs in front of them. If your garden is overlooked by an unpleasant view such as a factory you can always use the mirror remedy out of doors – and a mirror placed in the garden does wonderful things for opening up small spaces and making them look bigger.

▲ Use lilies in the wealth enrichment area of your garden to encourage the flow of money; according to the Chinese tradition they represent gold.

▲ Bamboo can be used successfully to screen garages, dustbin (trash can) areas and compost heaps. It encourages Ch'i with its movement in the wind.

48

GARDEN SHAPES

Draw up a Pah Kwa for your garden and see where the enrichments fall. You can then place your seat in the pleasure area, the swings in the children area, and so on.

You should also walk the Nine Palaces through your garden – and this should be done quite often even if you're happy with your finished garden, as the seasons change the look and feel of a garden. In the West most gardens are four-sided, and the two shapes you want to try to incorporate are the octagon and the circle. A feature such as a pond that is kidney-shaped or has a harsh irregular shape would be considered poor Feng Shui; circular ponds are better. The octagon shape is easy to incorporate with a little strategic repositioning of flower-beds.

The ideal shape is a square garden with flower-beds surrounding an octagonal lawn and a circular pond in the centre – with a fountain, of course.

▲ This traditional cottage benefits from rounded hedges as they encourage the Ch'i to flow harmoniously and gently.

◀ The paths encourage healthy Ch'i and the plants in pots can be moved around easily to help the flow of Ch'i in different seasons.

COURTYARDS

If you don't have a garden but just a small backyard you can still create an interesting and visually stimulating courtyard that will help the overall Feng Shui of your home. Courtyards are traditional in China but they are usually in a central position with the house built around them on all four sides.

Yours is more likely to be a yard at the back of your house. That is fine as long as you do not neglect it and just use it as a place to store the dustbins (trash cans). If the area is covered in concrete, cover it with gravel. With this more fluid material you can introduce curves to represent rivers, the sea-edge or even waves. Break up the square shape of your courtyard by filling the corners with pots, climbing plants or statues.

You could create an arbour by constructing a simple archway with plants growing up and over it. Arrange a seat under the arbour, perhaps a chamomile

▲ Paths don't have to have hard, straight edges; clever use of circular shapes helps the Ch'i to flow better.

▲ A small patio can be enhanced and the Ch'i can be invigorated by lots of plants in pots.

▲ Use lots of colour and curved beds in a dark corner to free up the Ch'i.

or thyme seat so that you can enjoy that heady smell.

Plant climbers in tubs to cover bare brickwork, or you could attach a wooden framework to the walls of the courtyard to support masses of pots of trailing plants, a wonderful and interesting way of gardening in a limited space.

Filling wooden tubs with herbs would be both good Feng Shui and useful in the kitchen. You could even incorporate a small fountain spouting in a gentle curve from a wall into a pool where it can be re-circulated. It takes up little space but brings move-ment, sound and life into an otherwise dead area.

The main thing to remember with a courtyard or backyard is not to neglect it. It should at least be swept regularly and kept tidy. And what enrichment does it fall in? This could be a valuable clue to any problems you are encountering in your life.

▲ To stop Ch'i stagnating in a long, thin garden, plants in containers provide curves and allow the Ch'i to circulate freely.

Check what the gates into your courtyard are made of – if they are metal and in the west try to replace them with wooden ones or the unpredictable Tiger Ch'i will be too strong.

PATHS AND ENTRANCES

The path to the front of your house is considered very important – it tells the world all about you.
Ideally it should curve gently, bringing your guests to you in harmony and health.

Too straight or direct a path or drive will channel your guests too quickly, and they will feel ill at ease when they reach your door. If the path meanders too much, however, your guests will arrive tired and bored. Entrances and paths benefit from having arches along them covered with climbing plants, but beware of thorny roses: their thorns are considered poor Feng Shui and are liable to harm your guests.

The shape of the entrance to your garden is important – what does it look like? If it widens too much Ch'i will leak away. If it narrows too much Ch'i will be trapped. If it is too harsh or angular the Ch'i will be disruptive. A horseshoe shaped drive or entrance is good as it allows the Ch'i to arrive gently into your home and eventually be channelled away when depleted.

▲ Paths can be used if you don't have streams or rivers; they encourage the Ch'i.

◀ If the Ch'i is allowed to flow gently into the house it will bring harmony and peace.

TREES AND FENCES

Trees in the garden are considered essential to good Feng Shui, but there are some principles to apply. Fences should be of natural materials and harsh, straight lines should be avoided.

Don't have trees that need radical pruning – anything that needs lopping off at the top will bring misfortune. Old trees, especially if they are gnarled, should never be removed – they've been there longer than you and their Ch'i is very powerful – don't interfere with it.

Never plant a tree directly in front of your front door as it will block the arriving Ch'i. Unless you live in a mountainous region, avoid pines and conifers. The ideal trees are willows, maples, apples and magnolias. Be wary of trees that are going to grow too big and overshadow your house, especially any trees planted to the west of your house – tigers just love to sit and wait to pounce in them!

Try to avoid changing the natural shape of any tree – it should be left to spread naturally.

▲ Attention should be paid to the earth element centre of the garden; here a tree and stillness remedy have been used to good effect.

◄ Trees planted too close to the house will prevent the Ch'i from entering the home.

► Use unusual natural materials for fences to avoid straight lines.

WATER

There is not a garden in the world that would not benefit from having a pond or pool in it – even a shallow protected one if you have children.

Moving water in the garden is excellent Feng Shui. A small fountain is easy to install and pumps are cheap. Water encourages wildlife and brings a garden to life; it also refreshes the Ch'i and soothes the nerves.

Ponds should be raised so that you can sit around the edge. Construct one in your money enrichment and fill it with goldfish to encourage wealth. If you do have a pond, make sure it is kept very clean and never allowed to stagnate or collect leaves in the autumn –

this can both harm the aquatic life and cause your own Ch'i to stagnate.

A succession of pools that empty into each other is considered very good as it allows Ch'i to both circulate and accumulate.

Garden centres sell a vast range of pond "furniture", but you should use only natural materials such as stone, bamboo or wood. Anything made of plastic is considered poor Feng Shui.

▲ A circular pond encourages the Ch'i to circulate freely and is excellent in a north-facing garden.

▶ A fountain refreshes Ch'i and
    is excellent in a south-facing
    garden for generating money.

ROCKERIES AND CLIMBERS

A garden should reflect the ideal layout of a home, with steep mountains to the north, gentle hills to the east, water to the west and open areas to the south. So if you have a pond in your garden, ideally in the west, the rockery should go to the east.

Rockeries should be planned deliberately and not be used to camouflage piles of leftover stones, and they should look as natural as possible. You can also incorporate the element of Wood into your rockery in the form of driftwood or ancient branches.

Climbing plants are very good Feng Shui as they allow Ch'i to fall and recirculate in the garden as well as being pleasant to look at. They are also excellent for hiding dustbins (trash cans) and the like, as well as providing hidden areas so the whole garden can't be seen in a single glance. Climbers along fences and walls can include roses as they are considered good for keeping out intruders (the thorns can be useful here).

▲ This bold clematis breaks up the harsh lines of a brick wall and provides a good colour remedy.

◀ Use a rock garden to help slow down Ch'i that is accelerating and to provide colour remedies.

▶ Climbers help break up the straight lines of corners and roofs as well as providing colour and life remedies.

FENG SHUI AT WORK

The rules governing Feng Shui at work are no different to those you use at home. First draw up a ground plan of your office, shop or factory. Overlay the Pah Kwa and see where everything falls. This can be an illuminating process. You may find your employees' rest area in your money enrichment or your cash register in your pleasure enrichment.

In the context of work, the relationship enrichment would apply to your business contacts and partnerships; the children enrichment would apply to new projects or contracts; friends, ideally, would be your employees; and the health enrichment should correspond to your rest area. Fame and wealth remain the same.

If you work at home then you'll need to check where you've put your work area - ideally in your wealth enrichment and not in your pleasure enrichment (unless you really enjoy working). A successful actor might rehearse scripts best in his fame enrichment, for example.

◀ A crowded and cluttered office layout such as this one will cause confusion and unease in work colleagues.

▶ Modern office buildings can be very cold and unwelcoming.

BUILDINGS AND ENTRANCES

The ideal location for your office or shop is on a corner, with the entrance and reception area cutting diagonally across the corner. This not only gives you more space for the entrance but also allows all that Ch'i to funnel customers in.

Check what buildings you have around you. Tall buildings to the west will provoke the unpredictable Tiger and cause your business to fail unless you remedy it with mirrors - use concave ones to make the buildings appear smaller. Tall buildings to the north are protective and good.

You should be wary of any stairs or escalators that are directly facing your main entrance: Ch'i will escape down them and take both your money and your customers with it.

▲ This curved building is less threatening than a building with sharp edges and the reflective glass throws off any unwanted negative Ch'i.

Make sure your reception area is spacious and welcoming. Plants (with rounded leaves to represent money) are good to encourage customers.

SITING A NEW BUSINESS

If you are looking for a new site for an office or shop you should tour the immediate area and make sure that the locale is prosperous and healthy - any closed businesses or derelict buildings are bad Feng Shui and you should avoid the area.

Look at the road immediately outside your building. Is it like a good Feng Shui river - curving towards you bringing luck, fortune, Ch'i and customers? Or is it arrowed at you (bringing killing Ch'i)? Roads pointed directly at your business are not good as they accelerate the Ch'i too forcefully. Any business in a dead-end or cul-de-sac will suffer from stagnating Ch'i and could well fail to flourish. The ideal site is where two or three roads intersect and you have the corner position, with any fast Ch'i running down the side of your building rather than straight at you.

▲ The smaller office buildings in the foreground could be threatened by such tall buildings behind.

◀ This office block has been built on new land and appears vulnerable as there are no other buildings around it to give it shelter.

OFFICE SPACE AND SHAPE

If you have your own office within a building it makes sense to overlay the Pah Kwa on to a floor plan of it and make sure that each enrichment is correct. Your desk should be in the south/south-east section as this is where you will make your money and reputation.

If several people share an office the desks should be arranged so that they form an octagon (or part of one) rather than having the desks in straight lines.

You have to spend a lot of time in your workplace so it should be as tasteful and harmonious as possible. No-one should be made to sit with their back to a fellow employee nor should they have to look at large blank walls; they should be decorated with pictures of beautiful landscapes (the Chinese use scrolls with calligraphy but you may prefer watercolours).

Doors and windows should open outwards to allow the Ch'i free access. If they open inwards you can put a small mirror on to the wall they face when open.

Mechanical devices can play too important a role in offices. The plethora of computers, telephones, photocopiers and fax machines can leave workers feeling drained and irritable by the end of the day. You can try hanging wind chimes to add sound and movement as remedies, but a small fountain would recharge the Ch'i better than anything else.

Colour schemes should be kept bright and clear. White is a good working colour, while pale blues will produce a calm atmosphere. Use red only if you are sure you can cope with all the extra energy it will generate. Any dark or unused corners should be lit with lamps and any sharp corners rounded off with plants. Keep "piped" music to a minimum as it is another remedy – and you may well not need it.

▲ The workers here have their backs unprotected and have no view. This will not make a happy workforce.

◀ This man, working in an open-plan office, has his back to the door and will be nervous of people coming up on him from behind.

BAD OFFICE LAYOUTS

GOOD OFFICE LAYOUTS

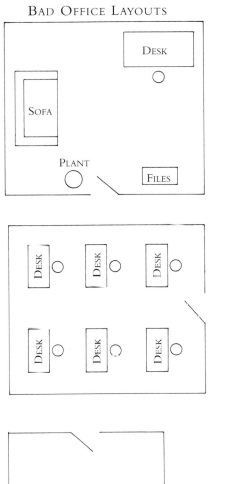

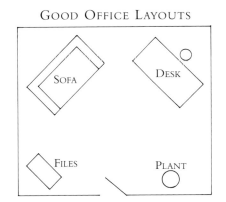

Desks where people sit with their backs to the door are considered bad Feng Shui.

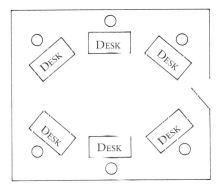

If you have a large pool of desks it is better to arrange them so that everyone can see the door and also to incorporate the Pah Kwa shaped.

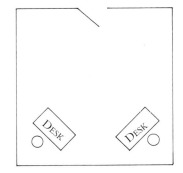

It is better to rearrange the desks so that each person faces the door.

DESKS AND WORKSTATIONS

The really important Feng Shui rule is never to sit with your back to the door when you are working. The reasoning behind this is you will never be able to relax and concentrate if someone could come up behind you without you knowing they were there. If there are two doors into your office you should position your desk so that you can see both doors.

▲ Ideally, your desk should face south/south-east to attract fame and fortune. Watch the size of your desk as well – if it is too large you'll feel swamped; too small and you'll feel restricted.

If you cannot have your desk facing the door and have to position it facing a wall, you should make a mirror remedy by placing a mirror so that you can see the door's reflection from your desk.

You can sit with your back to a window unless it faces west. If it does and you are obliged to sit that way round, you should have a blind at the window or a mirror facing outwards.

Organizing your Desk

Overlay the Pah Kwa on your desk. The front, where you sit, should be regarded as your fame enrichment. Keep your keyboard or notepad here. To the left is your health area, so it is advisable to keep your "out" tray here. This will help you to relax as each project is finished. To the right is your money enrichment – keep your "in" tray here and may it always be full.

Immediately opposite you at the back of the desk is your relationship enrichment – this is the place for your telephone. Immediately to the right is your children enrichment – a good place to keep a family photograph to remind you who you are doing it all for. To the left is your friends enrichment – a good place for your computer's processing unit where all your files (friends) are stored. The left-hand edge of your desk is your pleasure enrichment – here you can keep your coffee and cakes. The right-hand edge is your education enrichment, so this is a good place for reference books.

If you use a different kind of workstation, such as a work bench, reception area or whatever, you should do the same thing with the Pah Kwa and arrange your personal space accordingly.

▶   It is best to angle furniture to reflect the Pah Kwa shape and encourage the Ch'i to flow more harmoniously around the room.

▲ Try to avoid arranging furniture in straight lines or along walls.

INDEX

ACKNOWLEDGEMENTS

The publishers would like to thank the following libraries for providing pictures for this book: Peter McHoy pp 46, 47, 48, 49, 50, 51, 52, 53, 54; Zefa Pictures pp 6, 7, 9, 10, 13, 15, 16, 17, 18, 19, 20, 21, 22, 25, 43, 44, 56, 57, 58, 59, 60, 62, 63; The Hong Kong Tourist Association for the picture of the Feng Shui compass on p 12.